**Published by:** Write It Out Publishing, Inc. in the United States of America.

**Edited by:** Yvonne Ruffin

**2nd Edited by:** Tamira Butler

**Cover Design by:** Andre Mason

**ISBN-13:** 979-8-9874539-0-2

**Distributed by:**

Write It Out Publishing LLC

Virginia Beach, Virginia

writeitout@gmail.com

757-276-3640

www.writeitoutpublishing.com

Andre Mason

# FREEDOM PAPERS

*An Entrepreneurs Guide to Freedom*

Write It Out
PUBLISHING, LLC

VIRGINIA BEACH, VA

*An Entrepreneurs Guide to Freedom*

# Freedom Papers

ANDRE MASON

CONTENTS

## DEDICATION

To Alou & Wanda Lee. I pray I've made you proud. To Ciara and my three B's. I love you, these pages now seal that truth in eternity. To God, thank you, have your way.

# Tanika B.

Andre provided us with a one-day seminar that walked us through the process of establishing a business, gave us hands-on experience with designing and creating shirts, and even gave us guidance on websites to sell our products. He provided us with a beginning network that included business owners and an attorney. We were able to create and bring home a sample shirt at the end of the seminar, and he also provided us with clothing blanks for us to start our brand. Thank you, Andre, for your guidance and support.

# Kiyanni B.

The road to entrepreneurship can come with a lot of uncertainties. Unsure of when to start, the first steps, and anxious about the flow of income. In times like these you need the wisdom and support of someone who not only has taken the journey but they have compassion for what is not easily understood. Andre was that for me. He was a clear, sober, and focusing voice in my life at defining moments that left me in distress. I appreciated the encouragement, the guidance, and the prayers of his expertise. Because of him I stayed the course.

# William T.

Andre helped me to see something I didn't see in myself.

He helped give me the vision I needed to succeed in business. He provided a safe space for me to communicate with him about life. He always had my back and believed in and prayed for me.

PREFACE

# Freedom: (noun) the power to or right to act, speak or think as one wants without hindrance or restraint.

Words have power. Power to build, power to tear down, power to empower and invoke change. That power is equally present when you read *words on the paper, define them,* and especially when you say them. Thing is, it's possible to shout and profess all day that you are a thing and still not know how to truly become who and/or what you say you are. This was my dilemma for years in Corporate America. I was in a place where I didn't belong and where I did not fit. I knew I was not supposed to be where I was, there was a future calling me, I just didn't know how to get there.

Living in the moment, I knew I had the desire to be free. I had the language and the mannerisms that would indicate freedom but was in a place of bondage and restriction. I was unable to be who I wanted to be, who I needed to be, and ultimately be the best version of myself. So, the message is this: No matter who you are and no matter where you are, you can decide to run to that beckoning beacon of freedom that lives in your heart. And that's precisely what I decided to do.

This started for me when I was laid off from a job that I was on for many years. I couldn't help but be excited. That moment was the beginning, birthing the wisdom that I will share here. The small investments I made, in addition to my faith, prepared me for something life changing. Somehow I knew it wasn't just for my life to change but for yours also. So, welcome to my journey, *Freedom Papers*. My prayer is that its contents will give you some guidance as you transition into your own personal place of freedom.

Harriet Tubman achieved freedom and thought it not robbery to go and rescue others. Allow me to be your Harriet Tubman throughout our time together here. The journey to proverbial freedom will be a lot easier if you're accompanied by someone who has navigated the path before.

My journey is now documented for you to refer to, and some of the bumps, bruises, and hiccups I received you can avoid because I share those too. Without further delay, I present to you, *Freedom Papers*.

CHAPTER ONE

# Building Better

I want to lead you, but before I lead you, I need you to trust that I have your best interest at heart. Before you trust me to lead you, it is important to know where I come from. My story is typical, or at least typical to me, but distinct as well in hindsight.

I am the youngest of three children born to a two-parent home in the '80s in Brooklyn, New York. During this time, if you knew anything about New York in the '80s, drugs, poverty, and broken family dynamics (just to name a few) were the norm. My parents are from two of the poorest cities in the United States and both grew up in large families with a multitude of siblings during the Civil Rights era. My upbringing existed abnormally, or at least it seemed that way. Coming up, most of my friends were from divorced or single-parent households.

They were given what seemed to be more freedom while my world was a little more sheltered. While my counterparts were treated to the latest in fashion (even in the fourth and fifth grade) such as $100 Jordan's, Guess jeans, and whatever else was the latest trend, my apparel was much more subdued as I wore hand-me-downs (French Toast brand jeans and shirts, etc.).

I was teased for my ensemble when I transitioned from private to public school. I loved athletics and sports but also had taken a liking to less popular activities. Unusually athletic, I took a liking to gymnastics, and since I was musically inclined my mother introduced me to drum core as well.

Keeping in line with my aptitude for music and beats, I joined the step team and was recruited for my school's performing arts dance club, where I was introduced to the works of Alvin Ailey. Oddly enough, on the way to these places I would have to navigate the ugliness of a broken environment. Drug dealers, gangs, friends being shot or jumped, the daily threat of being robbed or beat, neighborhood shootouts and stabbings, etc. At every turn in the middle of the chaotic borough of Brooklyn, where you often hear war stories of brokenness, I was introduced to the beauty of its offerings and the culture. It was refreshing. I had teachers, tutors, and mentors that encouraged, cultivated, and pushed me. I attended gifted schools and programs from elementary to high school. As you can see, my activities were uncommon.

The summation of the matter is that I found myself to be overwhelmingly gifted in a multitude of areas, and if there was one thing that was not always celebrated in my social environment, it was shining brighter than normal and being a light unapologetically in a dark place.

I can see in hindsight the things I was teased for seemed to be some of the elements that are paramount in building the foundational theories and perspectives that cut the lens through which I view life today. My parents refused to pay thirty and forty dollars for clothes that were only worth five.

They were not poor, they were savvy. Giving away chunks of their paycheck for a brand name was not of interest to them. They equated the paycheck to their time, and, to them, the value of the garment did not warrant the exchange of that value. Instead, they gave us the option, "You want name brands? Then you get a job and spend your money on them." The echoes from my parents' voice still ring in my head.

My father, an analytical thinker and sponge for knowledge, has a viewpoint on life that literally will not allow him to waste. My mother, a relentless goal setter and goal-getter, does not see how making the rich richer could fit into the bigger picture of building a legacy. My mind, much too young to grasp the big picture, could not appreciate the fact that my siblings and I went without the latest fashions and the latest trends in exchange for the exposure and experience of having access to a summer home in Virginia.

The one thing that my friends and I had in common was the fact that we had hard-working parents who were working to provide a better life for their children. Where our worlds violently split seemed to be at defining what exactly "better" looked like. While my friends had the latest gadgets, games, material things, etc., we had exposure to the building blocks of legacy and longevity. The differences I was rejected for were the pillars that my bridge to freedom is built on today. Legacy, longevity, and value are all things that shape my decisions in my adult life.

Seeing that the connection may seem vague, let me try to button that concept up nicely for you. I experienced an extraordinary amount of rejection. I was an outspoken, gifted, short, buck-toothed kid from Brooklyn trying to fit in, but never did. Conflicted with whether to shine the brightest I could or to shrink back to blend with my environment, I've always shunned the latter. Blending, no matter how much I wanted to, was never going to work for me. It was never my forte. I did not come to accept the following truth until recently, but it has always been very obvious and apparent that I was built differently. Not always better, just different.

My differences will never allow me to fit into a mold or a make, and the same should be true for you. Our perspectives, our experiences, and our flaws all shape and mold unusual viewpoints that incubate farfetched dreams, imaginations, and plans. Are you like me? Are you noticeably different, or do you force your fit?

Brooklyn itself was a training ground. You can Google, ask an elder, or visit yourlocal library for microfilm or microfiche to verify that what I am saying is true. The concrete jungle had a way of applying pressure to the parts of your character that were not suitable to thrive in that environment. Early on, whatever I didn't get from the strict direction of my parents, I learned from the on-the-job training of being a kid in Brooklyn.

I learned how to navigate and conduct myself in dangerous situations. Situations such as a simple bus ride or walking to school every day, sidestepping the stick-up kids here, or spinning off the boosters and schemers there. It was a tightrope! Say the wrong thing, carry the wrong posture, or give off any signal of vulnerability, and that could catalyze a high-pressure situation.

At least, that is the way it felt to me. A dog-eat-dog world where you had to adapt, navigate, and get along the best you could. Every day was a risk. You could be met with some form of violence, the victim of a robbery, a bystander in the wrong place at the wrong time, or just plain old unlucky and meet with unfavorable circumstances a few blocks from your home or in some neighborhoods just a few steps from it.

The city had a way of cultivating an awareness that carried over into my adulthood. An ingrained discernment that makes you guarded against the intentions of men and women. One that beckons you to listen to what is never said and to search for the motive behind a movement.

It seemed like everywhere you went someone was looking to take advantage of you. I would be a fool to sit here and tell you that I was never caught in a snare or never a victim in that environment. The truth is though, I made it out of that place in one piece, and it is thanks to the great foundation I was given in and out of my home.

*Building Better:*

- ✓ Recognize the importance of sharing your journey.
- ✓ Acknowledge your differences while chasing your destiny.
- ✓ Honor your father and mother.
- ✓ Be grateful for where you came from.

Are you noticeably different, or do you fit in?

# TAKE TIME TO REFLECT

# TAKE TIME TO REFLECT

# TAKE TIME TO REFLECT

CHAPTER TWO

# Exposed

LOOKING BACK, I THINK THE EXPOSURE AND weekend trips to Virginia at our summer home are some of the most vital experiences in shaping who I am today. In New York, everyone was a hard worker, including my parents. The dream there was to get a good city job, a solid salary, and benefits. Perhaps I could work for the MTA like my mom or the Postal Service like my dad. That blueprint called for aspiring to 40-hour work weeks for 40 years until you retired. Having a car and an apartment or house in Brooklyn was it. All I wanted was a 40k/yr salary and a foreign car.

A BMW or Mercedes would suffice, but back in those days, my heart was set on an Infiniti Q45 with the big body, or maybe even the Acura Legend with leather and a sunroof (those were high hopes where I am from). I admire my parents for their work ethic and old-school values, but I wanted to be like my older cousins. The hustlers who shined. Some by legit means and some by not-so-legit means.

At an early age, they had acquired the stuff and hit the ceiling of what I had aspired to in New York, but even they fell short of what I saw when I went to Virginia for the summers. It was there that I would be exposed to my extended family, including my uncle David who lived in Emporia, VA. He would become a mentor of sorts later in my life, but as a kid I drew lessons by just watching him in action. I was able to experience life moving at a much slower pace in Emporia. It did not have the kill or be killed type of vibe or the win or go home urgency I felt every day in Brooklyn.

Heck, they did not have city buses, movie theaters, a bowling alley, or even an arcade. It was a town seemingly trapped in the '60s and '70s. People still waved to each other there and were polite, considering the courthouse had a confederate flag flying high and proud well into my teen years. We seldom saw any signs of what that flag represented in the people.

My grandmother and grandfather lived there, which exposed me to a house where fourteen kids were born and raised. A humble three-bedroom house that my grandfather built by hand. He was a pastor and had a radio show until health conditions put him in a near-vegetative state.

I was taken to the roots of my family every summer. The uncle I had the most interactions with during those summers was David. In hindsight, his impact can't be overstated. He is the first reference point I have for entrepreneurship. A brick mason by trade yet a jack of many other trades and almost master of them all.

He was always pleasant and welcoming, and he always sought to teach and not take. Brick mason during the week and a pastor on the weekends, he lived life on his terms. He did not punch a clock but worked with his hands to create the vision he saw in his head for himself and others. Uncle David was not interested in a job unless it was his job. Come to think of it, most of my uncles on my mother's side did not have jobs. They are mostly contractors or clergy, with a few exceptions. David navigated both, and he worked hard every day. He convinced my mother and father to purchase the summer home in Emporia, and it was him who exposed my mom to the wonders of real estate.

See, Uncle David wasn't just a brick mason. He took what he knew and built over twenty units for himself to rent for passive income, and he did so a little at a time with cash out of his pocket. He would build houses and sell them to his friends and family. Not just so that he could get rich, although I am sure that was a sweet byproduct of the arrangement. He did it so they could be introduced to investing in something that could live beyond them, that could pay college tuition for their kids, and that could generate income while they slept.

My uncle David's blueprint had exceeded in efficiency that of the hustlers I was exposed to, because the hustler's story lacked longevity, it lacked a legitimate exit that didn't involve a cell, a hospital, or a casket, and the opportunity costs were too high. His blueprint exceeded that of the working man, which requires you to trade your best years for someone else's dream, which till this day seems absurd. Uncle David's blueprint could be scaled, modified, and made more efficient (automated even).

Most importantly, Uncle David's blueprint gave him the luxury and flexibility of time, the freedom to do what he loved the most, and that is to do the work of the ministry helping others through his church, Lifeline COGIC. It allowed him to carry the legacy of his father in his way, manifest heaven on earth, and do the work of the kingdom unapologetically.

Uncle David was the man! He never drove high-end cars and his house was modest, but he was the most liberated and wealthy man I knew at that point. Until he passed, he became the inspiration and the impact I did not know I needed. I gained a wealth of wisdom by just being present in the interactions between him and my parents. The business conversations breaking down the thought processes of the buyer and the seller as well as the builder and the owner. Those conversations and the experiences on job sites with them were my introductions to the freedom school of hard knocks. Those experiences allowed me to see that though the entrepreneurial route could be more laborious, its payoffs were exponentially larger than the one advertised in the Urban American Dream brochure. You know the one, get a job, get a family, get a house, and maybe after you work 40 years, you can do what you want. Yeah, that one is definitely not for me.

I suppose here is as good a place as any to highlight the overwhelming impact, be it positive or negative, that exposure to the unfamiliar can have on a person. Without those summer trips, entrepreneurship outside of the illegal forms I saw in my environment might be a farfetched theory. Being able to be in rooms that gave my young mind a reference point for better and language for who I would aspire to be was life changing. When I saw Uncle David, I got a glimpse of what I would want my professional life to look like, what I wanted to sound like. Untethered to a time clock, able to impact others, and to make unlimited money while I did it. Are you feeling stuck? Lacking language for exactly where it is the Lord is drawing you to? Try exposure. Visit, explore, uncover...new. New places, new people, new perspectives that feed the best parts of you. This can be through conversations, conferences, travel, etc. Once you arrive in the rooms, they will either draw or detract from the desire in your heart. Find the voice drawing you to more. Get exposed.

*Exposed:*

- ✓ Where you are is not where you will always be or where you always must be.
- ✓ What worked in your lineage may not work for you.
- ✓ There is typically a point of reference that models what you desire.
- ✓ When were you exposed for the good and how did it change your life?

# TAKE TIME TO REFLECT

# TAKE TIME TO REFLECT

CHAPTER THREE

# A Different World

With those early exposures in consideration in my adolescent years, I had a general idea of the direction I wanted to take going into my teen and adult years. So, I took to the idea of wanting to pursue entrepreneurship, as I graduated from high school and enrolled at Hampton University to study business. My experience was not quite that of the folks that went to Hillman, but it was one worth documenting.

In this book, I will skip the details of my matriculation through junior high and high school, as it would no doubt be filled with awkward stories of my identity crises. The most relevant milestone would be Intro to HU, the illustrious Hampton University (Black Harvard). After receiving my acceptance, I was so excited. I was graciously given the opportunity to pursue a degree in business with my cousin Chap as my roommate.

It was perfect. I had received acceptance into the school of business in the entrepreneurship program and was too amped about the possibilities. I was sure of the direction my life compass had been pointing me to. I wanted to explore the theories I developed through encounters in Emporia and Brooklyn, and I was eager to learn. At least I was until I was blindsided by what I now will describe as a concerted attack against my destiny. My older brother had recently graduated from Hampton University, and I proudly walked in his footsteps to the gates of my home by the sea.

One of the advantages of that is I would be able to be introduced to some of the relationships that he had developed during his time there, and I welcomed the opportunity. It is move-in day, the dorm is set, and registration is next. My mother, father, and brother were talking with Dr. Jackson, at the time she was head of the Business program, although her exact title escapes me now.

The conversation went something like this, "Come here, Andre, I would like you to meet someone. This is Dr. Jackson."

"Hi, Dr. Jackson," I said eagerly, filled with excitement.

"Hi, Andre."

"Andre, Dr. Jackson says that you should reconsider pursuing entrepreneurship as a major and switch to the 5-year Master of Business Administration program. It is a great program."

"Well, why?" I inquired.

"Well, when you graduate it is likely to deter employers from hiring you. When they see your degree is in entrepreneurship, they will be less inclined to hire you because they will fear that you won't be there long term," said Dr. Jackson.

At the time, this seemed like conventional wisdom that would serve me well, so I switched. Did you catch that? Before I had taken any classes and before I had stepped foot on the road to the destiny that was in my heart, I had allowed the "wisdom" of another to derail me, detour me, and delay me. Why is this important to know? Well, because you need to know that distractions, detours, and derailments are sure to show up as threats (or even to intimidate you) as you try to start your journey.

In hindsight and at a closer view, this whole conversation should have been rendered null and void by one simple fact. I should not have cared about what employers would think because my goal was not to be employed but to be an employer. Entrepreneurship is not for those who wish to be a supporting cast member. I should have taken that advice with a grain of salt and kept on the path that my heart led me instead. I ended up starting an MBA but did not finish the program because I was not interested in it. It was not where my compass was pointing me.

Although I did graduate with a degree in Business Management, I now wonder, what if I would have stayed the course from the jump? What differences would there be in my life? Eighteen years later, I still remember that conversation, and eighteen years later, I find myself on the course that my heart was pointing me to from the beginning.

Dear reader, take my advice, your heart's compass is pointing you to that intended destination for a reason. It is not by happenstance nor is it by luck. You should now expect conversations, pseudo signs, or some other stimulus to come and try to take you off course. Instead of following, use it as a sign that you are on the right path.

Looking back, I would have stuck to my true north. I recommend that you never deviate from the course because of the opinions of others. If you do, I believe you will eventually navigate back to the proper course, but you will likely always wonder what beautiful things you missed while you were busy with your detour.

*A different world:*

- ✓ Do not allow the "wisdom" of another (even in its sincerest form) to derail, detour, or delay you on the road to destiny.
- ✓ Keep your eyes on your goal(s).

Follow the compass of your heart.

Describe a time when you've allow the "wisdom" of another to deter you from your goal and it didn't work in your favor.

# TAKE TIME TO REFLECT

# TAKE TIME TO REFLECT

CHAPTER FOUR

# The Plantation

Years passed and during my studies at the university, I had settled into the Business Management program. I became but a shadow of the once ambitious kid that entered into university. In hindsight, the decision to change majors that first day I grew to regret, and as a result I spent valuable formative college years in a spin, unsure of my place post-graduation, unengaged in the mandatory engineering classes that I was forced to take. Those courses stood towering as a masterpiece of irrelevance in the grand scheme of my goals. I remained unimpressed with my coursework until about my junior year. The management program was not the entrepreneurship program I originally intended to attend nor was it the MBA program that was recommended, but it was close enough. After graduation I landed a management position with Sherwin Williams, an international paint and coatings supplier. I was amped, having all of my entrepreneurial ambition thoroughly sedated through the bland curricula and perspectives at university. I was now singularly focused on achieving the "American Dream" through the traditional means. Excited to start a decent paying job with benefits, bonuses, and the opportunity to build someone else's dream. I know, I seem a little salty, but honestly, it was here where I learned about business in a day-to-day setting, so it wasn't all bad. I'm actually grateful for every day spent tinting paint, driving sales, and learning about how a business is run. Little did I know, this company would not only teach me much more than P&L and basic business principles, but it would also provide me with what now stands as my defining moment, a moment that would strip me of the sedative that I received at university, a moment that sounded a siren in my spirit. The moment that the voice that was silenced on that first day of university would again begin to speak, loudly. The message that voice echoed was…This ain't it.

Every year Uncle Sherwin (Sherwin Corporate officials) would treat the management and territory sales reps to a few days of R&R and teaching to prepare for the next year.

This particular year, a friend and I were able to meet the CEO of the company. Chris Connor, a well-seasoned executive who had led the company to record-breaking years in sales. "Hi, Mr. Connor, my name is Andre Mason. I run Store 5014. It is a pleasure to meet you," I said.

His face filled with a welcoming smile. As he reached in our direction to shake hands, a silent affirmation, it signaled to us that he welcomed the conversation, so we moved closer. Here was a chance to learn maybe the keys that would propel us to the next level. Who knows, maybe one day we could even have his job. Rell, my friend and mentor, introduced himself as well.

There we were, two Black men from the inner cities of America now holding court with a CEO from a Fortune 500 company. The setting was our annual corporate event, with thousands of employees from near and far, free-flowing drinks as far as the eye can see, commoners and power players all in one room.

Rell and I now had the attention of the most powerful man at the conference. Not one for wasting an opportunity, my friend, a high-performing manager in our district, went on to tell Mr. Connor about his phenomenal year. I was not so fortunate so I settled to be a fly on the wall in the interaction. I think Rell was walking the stage that year, which was a notable achievement reserved only for the company's high performers. As Rell gave Mr. Connor the rundown of his epic year, I watched intently and listened without interrupting. Little did I know, this moment would forever be etched into my memory, a defining moment of my dealings inside corporate sales, but perhaps not for the reason you think.

The allure of the moment would become muddied with one sentence from the most powerful man in the room. Soon after Rell finished running down his achievements over the past year, gleaming with confidence, he fell silent, awaiting Mr. Connor's reply. I was bursting with anticipation, thinking maybe Rell just got us some additional notoriety and an invitation to the private executive ball where we'd be afforded a glimpse into what all the big wigs did at the conference. I was expecting to hear an affirmation followed by some sound words of advice at least, but what followed was this: Mr. Connor smiled brightly with the pride of a first-time father, put his hand on Rell's shoulder, and said, "That is excellent, now go out there and make me some more money." I was crushed.

With that short reply, Mr. Connor, the company CEO, walked off, and with him went any notion that I may have previously led me to believe that the company I was working for, putting in long hours and giving my best for, actually valued me as a person. Probably close to a million dollars had to be spent to facilitate the corporate event that I stood in, but the bottom line for me was that the sentiment expressed by the company's leading man was the cold, hard, ugly truth. We were but a number.

Rell and I laughed it off, though we were fully aware of what happened. We did not dismiss it nor sweep it under the rug. It served as a silent confirmation of what we had already suspected internally, but I think we both processed the moment differently. Rell being from the south was used to the mentality that Mr. Connor displayed. It is a mentality akin to that of a master and slave interaction.

For the sake of not getting lost in the weeds with the comparison, I will stay away from the racial aspects of this. Allow me to state facts and input some acknowledgments here to counteract the loud but not very far-reaching voices of those criticizing the comparison as they read this.

Slavery was indeed involuntary, slavery indeed had harsher conditions and consequences. Slavery is an institution that has generational consequences, i.e., trauma, generational wealth gaps, and a still very present systemic racism that is seen everywhere from our legal system to our everyday interactions in covert and overt ways.

Those things considered, I still chose to use this institution as a comparative mentality because at its root we have a superior and inferior dynamic, a small group who benefits off the work of the masses, and a mass population who is left to compete for what is left over after the few have been fed.

This is one of the reasons I compare my time in corporate sales to plantation life. Field slaves are field reps. House negroes are managers. Regional managers as overseers, and vice presidents, chief operating officers, and chief executive officers as masters. Welcome to the plantation. For me, now close to ten years later, it is still one of the defining moments that started the shift in my mentality. From then on, I was crystal clear on who I was, where I was, and what I needed to do. The clarity I had when I arrived on campus that first day was restored. That one moment knocked the dust off a mentality I had put down for years. Thank you, Mr. Connor! It was clear, on this plantation I was just another number, a worker bee that could break records, but still, he looked at me as if I was average.

I started as a field Negro and graduated to the house Negro, but likely would never be an overseer lol. I was in a company that would consistently speak to the value of its human capital, going so far as to invest in the image to sell that dream, but at its heart only valued the production not the person. It was an insatiable beast, one that would take more than it could ever give. This is the truth in most businesses. You can tell because typically, the reward for good production is a demand for even better production the next year no matter the climate you're selling in. You have to find a way to feed the beast.

These realizations left me with the understanding of what I needed to do:

Leave this plantation, find a place where I could be fulfilled financially, not overburdened emotionally, and valued genuinely... Proverbial freedom.

This was just one of many encounters I had, each one tailored to push me to freedom in its own way. Until then, I had bought into the notion that I as an individual was of value to the company. The encounter with Mr. Connor would show me that my value was measured by how much I was able to produce (this is the nature of business and whether it is right, wrong, or indifferent, it is the truth.).

True as it was, this new perspective coupled with that encounter made the experience at that company unsettling and eventually unbearable. After a few more encounters with upper management that reinforced this truth, I became resolved in my mind that there were greener pastures to explore.

Some of those encounters birthed internal conflicts that were psychological while some were moral, but all pointed me to the knowing that where I was would not be it for me. I am tempted here to leave a few pages for you to write your encounters.So I've taken the liberty of doing so. While my story is fresh on the page, there may be a story that you have, similar to mine. Jot it down and answer the following questions in the pages provided below.

What are some of the things that are etched in your mind that let you know that where you are is not where you should be? If you could change it all today, where would you go? What would you be doing? Why? What is your purpose, your driver, your reason?

In the following pages, I have given you the space to come to terms with these questions. One thing I can tell you from where I sit now is that you will need them. As you journey to your proverbial freedom, there will be trials, tests, and attacks to navigate. Knowing the answers to those questions will be the only thing that keeps you focused.

So, start now while you have the chance, because it would be a mistake to try to figure them out in the wilderness.

The following chapters will be my attempt at explaining what I did from this point, why I did it, and what I learned along the way. If you have not decided that where you are is not where you should be, then this information will have very little value to you.

If you, like me, have noticed some similar behaviors where you are, and have decided that you must change, and that you are willing to die doing so, then what is to come in the following chapters will be a map of sorts for your journey. The words are the landmarks, and they won't just direct your feet, but they will become a compass for your soul. I will see you on the other side. Good luck.

# TAKE TIME TO REFLECT

# TAKE TIME TO REFLECT

CHAPTER FIVE

# Want to Escape: Build a Bridge!

SOME PEOPLE MAY NOT UNDERSTAND how difficult it is to work feeling undervalued, but the offense grew heavier once I started to calculate the proposition presented in my mind. The argument presented itself as follows: Said company gave me a budget. Let's just say the company's expectation was for my store to generate one million dollars in sales per year. If I successfully generated one million dollars, my reward in compensation would not even amount to 10 percent of the company's earnings per year in salary.

My logic starts to inform me that I am getting the short end of the stick because the salary in proportion to the value and revenue I produce then seems lopsided. This serves only as the root. I began to feel taken advantage of, and to think, I spent 44 to 48 of my hours per week doing heavy lifting, meeting/selling customers, setting up accounts, managing the inventory, and settling credit disputes. All of this while not receiving at least 10 percent of what I was generating began to make me feel overwhelmingly cheated.

Beyond that point, bonuses at the company that once satisfied me no longer made me feel whole financially. I could not get over the thought that I was not being compensated for all the work or the amount of production I was providing the company. I convinced myself that the value I was creating and being assessed on was not in line with what I was receiving. This train of thought would soon birth a preoccupation with evening the odds.

As a wise old delivery man said, "I want the Lion's share."

It was time to move on! I had enough mistreatment, undervalued compensation, and long hours to last for a lifetime. Besides, the voice I had silenced was now speaking louder than ever. My nights were starting to get more and more sleepless. Therein lies the answer to one of the most common questions those who desire to transition have.

The question is, how do I know it's time to leave? I would be lying if I told you I had all the answers, but what I do know is that one of the main signs that it is your time to go is when you are fed up, truly fed up with where you are, it will pain you to stay. You will no longer be able to justify it logically, you will no longer be satisfied with a piece of a piece, and you will want the Lion's share. If you align with this thinking, well, my friend, it's possible that you are being strongly signaled to make a change. To escape where you are and to set course for where you need to be.

I needed a plan. One that would help me transition with no conflict of interest to where I was, but still paved a clear, profitable direction to where I wanted to be. My plan to escape was simple... use what was in my hand to get to where I wanted. I looked around and it became so clear. I had access! Access to people, access to resources, and access to a secure salary that I would now use to fund my escape.

The goal?

Create a self-sustaining system that would be so effective at providing revenue that it would not matter if my regular job came or went. It would not matter if I got up to go to work or if I stayed asleep all day. The formula for my plan was one part real estate, one part cleaning company. Yes, I was set. The real estate part seemed to be the most simple and natural fit seeing that it is a family business, this was an ode to what my parents and my uncle David had shown me to be an easy entry point to entrepreneurship and wealth. So at that point, the biggest hurdle became financing. I found out that I could take a loan from my 401k without being penalized and pay myself back, and that's just what I did.

So, as opposed to using credit, I used my own funds to acquire my first property (allow me to insert one of the most vital keys to success that I learned in the search to finance my deal). It was subtle in that example, so I will accent it here for your benefit. The lesson is simple and can be applied universally. Information is key. Information is powerful, but it is only dangerous and a catalyst to the success of those who apply it. Success does not belong to the strongest nor the smartest, it belongs to those who hold and apply the most relevant information. If I hadn't researched and come to understand the immediate benefits of my 401 then I might struggle to find financing through other channels.

Many people are well informed. Some use it solely to display bravado. Typically using what they have learned in intellectual exercises at social gatherings much to the disdain of some and the applause of others. Truly, it is the ones who apply what they learn who become the leaders and pioneers of tomorrow. The spoils go to ones applying the information they attain not the ones just reciting it. Let's put this in the context of someone attempting to run to freedom. I imagine there are two types of people that chose to run for freedom.

***Type 1:*** These people want freedom with all their heart and soul and have decided to run, but once they get started, they stumble into a wilderness without any resources and any direction, they make an uninformed decision to run. These type one individuals are driven by desire, zeal, and adrenaline. They start with great intentions and are likely impulsive, neglecting to count the cost of the journey, or to research the destination. As a result, when they reach the wilderness, they become fatigued mentally and spiritually. Eventually, if not caught in the snare of circumstance, they soon succumb to the curse of the ignorant and uninformed, they will wander!

This type of person would eventually get caught, maimed, and returned to where they started. As a result of a failure to plan, they may be discouraged from ever trying again. They convince themselves that freedom is not for them and will be so shell shocked that they will never attempt to run again.

***Type 2 is much like type 1.*** They want freedom with all their heart and soul and have decided to run, but before they do, they have counted the cost, they become informed and plant their expectations in firm foundation. They have plotted the way and at least know the general course they are going to take to achieve their goal. Of course, they understand that not every plan goes smoothly and are open to adapting to what curveballs are thrown along the way. A type 2 individual has a far greater chance of making it to freedom successfully. You and I should be no different.

Knowing that you want to escape is not enough, you'll also need an idea of what system you're going to use to escape. As my parents put it, if you fail to plan then you should plan to fail. I imagine pioneers that have an emancipator's spirit start with a plan. Moses, Harriet, and Martin, all had some idea of which way they were going to get to the proverbial and literal forms of freedom they were after. At the very least, the first few steps of a plan mapped out. You and I are no exception. Where are you going? How will you get there? Are there any systems in place that will make your journey easier?

Yes. For now you're in a place you cannot stand. You know there is a future that awaits you full of fulfilling moments and fulfilling work.

Will you be type 1 or type 2? Are you planning to run based on pure impulse and pure passion, or are you going to be the type 2 runner who uses impulse passion and information to reach your goal? In my synopsis, the question that begs to be answered here is: Are you running from something, or are you running to something? The type 1 person that is running based on his or her disgust from where they are coming from will find it feasible to settle anywhere if that place is not where they were. A person like a type 2 who is running to something will not settle until they have reached the place that was outlined in their plan. There is a difference.

One of these types (type 2), in my opinion, has a much greater chance for success. One is running to escape while the other is running to be free. Escape is achieved once you are in a different place than you were yesterday. An escape can come with a job change, exchanging one master for another, or even changing partners in a relationship. As long as where you are is different than where you were, you will count it as a success, but freedom requires a new level of independence. A literal shifting of states, and it supplies the one chasing it with fulfillment.

Freedom is not achieved until one has crossed over to the place that they have set their sights on. Escape requires desire. Freedom requires a plan. I am here to tell you that both type 1 and type 2 can make it, but it is my opinion that one of these has a greater likelihood of reaching the end that they are so desperate for. You need a plan!

The elements of my plan were simple and followed, for the most part, the S.M.A.R.T. format I learned from my former employer.

When making your plan, each element should subscribe to the following parameters:

**S.** Your goals should be specific and should answer the question of what is it that you want to do.

**M.** Your goals should be measurable and is typically a quantifiable way of knowing that you have hit your target. Answer the question of how much or how many. Set a quantifiable goal by which to measure your success.

**A.** Your goals should be attainable. Is your goal reasonable given your current resources and position?

**R.** Is your goal realistic? Set relevant and realistic expectations. Projecting sales to jump from zero to a million in six months in a marketthat you have no experience in may be a little farfetched, so anticipate hurdles and respect the process when setting your goals.

**T.** Your goal should be timely. Set a date or time by which you hope to achieve your goals. Use this as your guide when starting your plan and you will have a firm foundation to work with. In preparation for setting goals and deciding to save I began:

Writing out goals and numbers

Put myself on deadline

Another important piece to have in view as you plan your escape are reference points. A reference point by my definition, is a person or a place that resembles who you want to be or what you want to create. In most cases there's nothing new under the sun. So with that being said, there is or has been some form of what you want to produce already out there. If you can find it, or find them, if it's a person, then you will have the unique opportunity to study their successes and their shortcomings, what made them grow, what stagnated growth? All of this information you can download to your mental file and implement the information you get in the plan that you're putting together.

As a manager, I had a unique opportunity to this because my main client base was

individuals who already had achieved what I wanted to be, an entrepreneur. I began to poll the business owners, asking them if they would ever get a job. Why not? Why are you an entrepreneur? What would you do different if you started over? Every time I would receive a valuable response, I'd add it to my intel; one sticks out to me the most.

One day, I asked a guy named Mike my poll questions.

"Mike, why don't you get a regular job and work for someone else?" He responded very simply, "I have never seen a millionaire on a W2."

It struck my heart! That stays with me to this day. Although this statement isn't an absolute truth because there are indeed a few who've made it to millionaire status on a company salary. He was explaining to me that he wanted to be a millionaire, and for the majority of us, this wasn't going to happen at someone else's company. That goal could not be achieved by working for someone else and working under someone else. At the time my goal was not to be a millionaire, but the sentiment was not wasted on me. I did want to be financially independent with an abundance of time to come and go as I pleased. At the time I looked around at my colleagues and higher-ups, the sad truth was I would never meet that goal with a W2 as my sole source of income at my age, at least not without outside investments. Although it is very well possible after reaching retirement age to have a million dollars, the prospect of waiting until 65 to get to freedom just isn't for me. I knew then that I needed to begin my transition.

Another element that became valuable in formulating my transition, was a shift in the way I viewed where I was. After the meeting I found myself very displeased, even depressed with where I was career wise, but I was overlooking the fact that I had been stewarding some very profitable resources in the form of my contact list. I'd spent years developing relationships with decision makers at other companies on behalf of my employer, but what was stopping me from leveraging the relationships I had cultivated for myself? Answer: Nothing! It is often said that a network is a net worth, and the same is true when starting a business. Instead of trying to be a real estate mogul overnight or come up with some witty idea, I received the divine insight to use the network I already had so that I could use relationships already established to build a company. I did not have to search for prospects because I already had several complexes and properties I already worked with before on paint jobs.

I had already built relationships with key decision makers, making it so that I did not have to advertise. All I had to do was ask. No longer would I exchange time for money at my normal job, now they would have to pay me with their clients as well. My mentality became, what the company has is now mine. Mi casa es su casa, or my home is your home.

Hey reader, what resources can you leverage to help you get started? Is there a contact list, a stage manager, or a decision maker that your day-to-day interaction through your normal job has allowed you to build a relationship with? Are you privy to a process that you can leverage to create a complementary, not competitive, offering? Look at where you are, look past your disdain, and look at it with fresh eyes. Answer this question, how can where I am help to serve where I want to go?

For me, the company resources became my resources. The company clients became my clients. The company tools became my tools. The company hustle became my hustle. During this time, God began to prick my heart about starting a cleaning company. He began to teach me principles about how to build the company because I did not know anything about cleaning. I would hear stories from entrepreneurs, but I had relationships with maintenance professionals. One of these professionals was Chris and he gave me the idea.

Chris was a local maintenance guy for one of my accounts. He would-willingly share the information I needed about payments and overall, how the system worked. He explained that his complex averaged about 30 turns every three weeks. He let me know that his management company was currently paying a cleaner $100 for a unit and a painter $400 for a unit. I could not believe the numbers; they far exceeded the money I was making as a manager. I would only need a portion of their business to make my financial goals. I could work less but make more.

Honestly, I sat on this information for some time due to having a lot of anxiety about going into a new field. It seemed a little too good to be true, and I figured an opportunity with less resistance and barrier to entry would arise. One that would allow me to learn the game on training wheels as opposed to being thrust into it. Sure enough, a few months later Chris came into the store, and I was presented with an opportunity to do about 26 hallways twice a month for about $500 each. Perfect! I gathered a team, set aside my fears, and began to transition to freedom.

One of the most valuable principles I took away from the start of the journey was this: Instead of jumping out there and trying to build something from scratch, patiently build a bridge from where you are to where you want to be. Rome was not built in a day, and the journey from bondage to freedom typically will not happen overnight. What I am saying is typically, these things take time. Most people when they decide to transition from where they are to where they want to be, convince themselves that the transition must be swift.

That, in my opinion, would be a lapse in judgment. Though sometimes quitting cold turkey may be the only way to maintain your dignity, or the best way to not catch a case, I would venture to say that the more patient approach will prove better in the long term. Building a bridge to freedom very simply means that you will use what you currently have at your disposal to resource your escape. I worked in the paint market, but instead of starting a hair salon, I used my experience in that industry to build the foundations of my escape plan.

Prospective clients, industry information, and chances to offer my services were all made available by simply adjusting my approach to what I was already doing. Let's take a moment to take a look at what is in your hands... Where are you currently working? What do you do there? No job? What skill set has been cultivated in your work historically? Who is in your network? How can you slightly adjust your approach to serve your transition? Now,let's be clear, I am not encouraging you at all to steal, cheat, or operate in the realm of any illegalities.

I am simply asking you how you can augment your approach to your everyday work to better serve your personal goals. In that next client meeting, after your presentation, during informal chatter, can you probe the target on whether they would be interested in a closely related service? Are you able to ask industryinsiders what types of services they feel are missing? Get creative.

In the space provided, answer some of these questions for yourself and quickly map out how where you are can serve where you are looking to go.

Your environment should begin to benefit you just as much as you benefit it. Break out of the mindset of exchanging time for money. Realize that there is more to be leveraged there. Look closely!

I had taken Chris up on his offer and after a year or so, I had gotten the hang of running a business part-time while working full-time, but that was not the extent of my plan; it was only the first phase. Part two would be trying my hand at a proven path to passive income: real estate. More specifically, a buy-and-hold rental property. If my numbers served me correctly, with my current income from the cleaning company, plus my income from the paint store, all I needed was one or two properties to be set.

So, I repeated the process. I looked for what was in my hand and who was in my network. I did not have to look far. I spoke with my mother and let her know my plan was in motion. She agreed to help, and it was that simple. I am aware that I made that sound easier than it may have been, and you may not have access to an individual in the industry you are looking to infiltrate, but I am pretty sure you've got access to YouTube, Instagram, or Google.

Count them in your network as well. Getting hung up on what resources you do not have available is not the way to get to the next place. Your mentality should be to play the hand you were dealt and to leverage the relationships you do have to win. I digress, the plan was to take money from the 401k, purchase a beat-up property, and renovate it for monthly cash flow. If the first one worked out, then it would be as simple as rinse and repeat.

The process to acquire my first investment property was a fairly smooth one. This is solely because I had something that most of us don't openly welcome. Mentorship, I had someone to guide me into rooms and through spaces that I did not have any experience in. My mother's mentorship in real estate made my transition into it seamless. The second element that made it an easy play was my willingness to research outcomes, processes, financial requirements, etc., before I jumped into a new venture. In short, I learned. Dear reader, I can't emphasize enough that desire alone is not going to carry you into your next. The little voice that you hear calling you out of a place is not just a signal that greater is coming, it's an invitation to learn as much as you can about where you're going as well. Information will empower you if you let it. Trust me, learn all you can before you execute your plan to escape so that your willful ignorance will not be the reason that success eludes you. Get a mentor, learn and remain teachable. You're new to this transition, supply yourself with every benefit possible through the technology of education and information. Invest in courses, take a prospective mentor to lunch, binge watch tutorials on YouTube. Whatever you have to do to get ready, DO IT!

Sure, the plan sounded great in theory, but there were also those pesky fears and anxieties I had to overcome to make the simple first step of getting off the plantation mentally. Luckily, years and years of repressed emotion fueled the fire and gave me exactly what I needed to run. From the start to the finish of this first step, it took me about three to four years.

It was by no means an overnight success. By the time I had acquired my first rental property and started a cleaning business, I had also received a promotion. I was able to have more flexibility in my time. I had hit a great stride and life was going SWEET! I had settled at this point. I had a business going part-time and rental property that was cash flowing. I had achieved a rare, sweet spot that I and a few had tasted. Being able to create my own schedule on the corporate dime while simultaneously taking in revenue from passive sources.

I loved every minute of it. But soon the inescapable truth confronted me face to face. The promotion I got at the job had only afforded me a new master with more lenient living quarters, but it had not afforded me the freedom I so desperately wanted. I was type 1 fronting like I was a type 2. I had settled, I started to run but had only upgraded my master. The truth is, even though I had a plan, I had not executed it to full capacity.

I was not free; I was just pretending to be. On no day was this clearer than when I received what I felt was an unction from the Lord that said very simply: It is time to leave your job. What would you do if someone told you to quit your job a few months after you bought a new house? Would you think they were crazy? Off? How would you feel about that? Because that is what happened to me.

2016 was coming and I was feeling in the pit of my stomach to quit my job. But it was not logical, it did not make sense, and it would be downright irresponsible for me to do so with all that was going on at that time. I had just closed on a house. I had a good thing going, so clearly it could not be the Lord to abruptly interrupt the flow. I found this line of thinking to be far from true. I went to a trusted voice, an elder that I knew could hear God clearly, and asked him what he thought about some of the thoughts I had about what I know God told me.

I was told that it cannot be God, that it was not logical, and it overall was not a good idea. After that conversation, I felt a sense of relief. Now, I knew that I was being crazy, and he was just the cosign that I needed to fuel my doubt. His insight kept me right where I was at. This turned out to be the birthing place of one of the simpler lessons I learned in the process: Just because a voice is more seasoned does not mean it is always accurate.

A few weeks later the company with which I worked for seven years acquired a new company and sent out an email telling everyone to stay home. A few days later, a few people got emails to come into the office, myself included. It was a Thursday when I walked into the office and was greeted in a meeting by someone I did not know and had never met. The unknown man placed the call on speaker phone, and said to the voice on the other end, “Hi, I have Andre Mason here in the office.” The voice on the phone responded, “Hi Andre, I am John.”

The summary of what followed is that the company was letting me go. In case you missed it, I was being fired, over a speaker phone, by a stranger, on a random Thursday. The company I had sown years of my life and time into did not have the decency to even cut ties in an honorable fashion. I have got to be honest, I expected nothing less and to some, this may sound like a bitter rant, but you would be mistaken.

I am simply stating the facts and if it sounds dry, cold, and callous, then that is because it was. I was given a severance package and told how much I was worth by a gentleman that did not know me when he explained my package to me. I made a video as soon as I walked out of that office.

It is called *"OMG I JUST GOT FIRED, NOW WHAT."* I was calm and collected, ready to go full force into whatever was next. To this point, because I had been building the bridge to where I wanted to be, this event didn't really bother me. I had recalled the conversation with Mr. Connor, I looked at the prospects from my side business and came to terms with the truth that I had settled and knew I had a decision to make. The next day, a former client who had heard the news had reached out to offer a job. There I was again, faced with the decision on whether or not I would upgrade my master or be a full-time entrepreneur.

I chose the latter. It took about a month to map out my plan to move forward. I became aggressive about advertising and transitioning to full-time entrepreneurship with new work ethic and diligence. I began to pursue real estate because it was something I always wanted to do. I worked in my cleaning business, and all was flowing very nicely from mid-2017 through 2018. I had some rentals and picked up another complex to clean.

I had a theory:

If I could create a self-sustaining system where several income streams feed off each other to keep the current and flow of all functions, then I'd be fine. When this currency runs smoothly, I could build and stack money. If an emergency comes up, I would be able to fill in the gap without breaking the momentum. This system, when set up right, can heal itself and could keep me financially grounded. It seemed foolproof until mid-2018 when literally every one of my income streams was stifled.

One of the first things to happen was a series of checks being held. These checks were from property management companies and complexes I did work for. These checks would come every 30 days or so and now they were being held with no explanation as to why. The stretching out of the checks threw off the pay cycles, and every system I had in place for making payments was abruptly interrupted. The system was now toppled. This left me stuck!!!

The bills including the mortgage were not able to be paid, and this caused a domino effect of financial strain and hardship. The checks would be held anywhere from 30 to 90 days at that time. If you've been adulting for any amount of time, you know that the bills come every thirty days and that the collectors never take a pretty face or an excuse as payment. The next challenge came with tenants from my property that did not pay their rent on time, and/or bailed out on their payments and lease, leaving me with a vacant property in the middle of the night. Before I knew it, my perfect plan began to haveholesin it. Several holes in the system caused the full-time entrepreneurship boat to begin to sink. By the time we hit 2019, the whole system was completely crushed. Work had dried up, bills were still due, and I became overwhelmingly stressed and discouraged. It is not hard for you to imagine the emotional turmoil that accompanied this sudden turn of events. When I started the journey I had only allowed myself to plan for a rainy day, but now, what seemed like a tsunami or monsoon had come my way, and I was struggling to make sense of it all.

Let's just say anxiety, depression, and stagnation were all on the visitors list as I served time in an emotional prison. I tried to trust that things were going to work out, but honestly, most days I felt like I was out here looking crazy. My wise counsel all signaled for me to abandon my dream, my ideas, and my goals, and for a while that sounded like the right thing to do. In hindsight, the truth that I can see so clearly now was not always as readily apparent in the moment, but this difficulty opened my eyes, birthing a much-needed moment of clarity. My friend, as you read this, I need you to understand that even the most perfect plan can and likely will be hit with a wave of unforeseen, impromptu tests and obstacles. I'd like to say that the nest egg that you have set to the side for a rainy day will be enough. But I sense that what's more important for you to know is that the obstacles you'll encounter are intended to stretch you and they should be embraced, not resisted. These types of experiences are the ones that act as the separating place. The question that begs to be answered is, what is your truth? Typically, the answer to this question lies in the center of a difficult place, the place I call the wilderness.

# TAKE TIME TO REFLECT

# TAKE TIME TO REFLECT

CHAPTER SIX

# The Wilderness

AS TIMES GREW MORE DIFFICULT I came to understand that something had to be done fast to stop the financial hemorrhaging that my family and I had been experiencing. Although, instead of a job, I decided to pursue other means of income outside of the traditional structure. It was liberating. My emotions ran the gamut from excitement and anxiety to confusion and loneliness. I did odd jobs for family, began to Door Dash, and worked diligently to get my rental property occupied with a tenant, all to keep my ship afloat. For the moment, I had to deviate from the plan.

It got me out of Egypt but wouldn't be enough to take me to Canaan. In the beginning, I indeed practiced what I preached. I made a plan and followed it, but I would soon come face to face with a very sobering reality. The truth is that any person that decides to obtain their freedom finds themselves at one time or another in a wilderness of sorts. I describe it as a wilderness because of its significance in scripture.

The wilderness is a separating place. Moses had one and so did Jesus. Sometimes the encounter takes place before you are even launched into destiny and sometimes you encounter it on the way. While you may think that the separation I described is a separation of you from others in your past, the truth is much more jarring.

The separation I am describing is a proverbial separation of you from yourself. What do I mean? The children of Israel had a promise over their heads. The promised land awaited all those who had the gumption and the desire to leave Egypt, but their desire alone didn't mean that they were prepared for their destination. For the first time in a few centuries, this nation was free from any sort of external bondage, but they were not yet ready to rest at their destination, not because of external factors but internal.

Exodus 13:17-18 King James Version

17 And it came to pass, when Pharaoh had let the people go, that God led them **not** through the way of the land of the Philistines, although that was near; for God said, Lest peradventure the people repent when they see war, and they return to Egypt: 18 But God led the people about, through the way of the wilderness of the Red Sea: and the children of Israel went up harnessed out of the land of Egypt.

Here is another translation that serves to make the point clearer and it comes from the New International Version of the Bible:

Exodus 13:17-18

17 When Pharaoh let the people go, God did not lead them on the road through the Philistine country, though that was shorter. For God said, "If they face war, they might change their minds and return to Egypt." 18 So, God led the people around by the desert road toward the Red Sea, a The Israelites went up out of Egypt ready for battle.

What is being suggested here is that the wilderness experience was prepared for Israel, not by their enemy, not by themselves, but by the one who had vowed to set them free, God. Can I submit to you that on the road to freedom, the physical move out of a place isn't the only sign of true freedom? What I am boldly suggesting is that freedom from bondage internally is also a thing that is of paramount importance to God himself. So important that he is willing to delay the manifestation of your success to ensure that you are fortified enough internally to sustain it. Why? Simply because if you were ushered into the place you desired today, without your wilderness, there are things on the inside of you that would cause you to forfeit the place that God himself has prepared for you. What does that look like? Well, for many of us this may look different. It may manifest in a quietly nagging insecurity about your stature or your educational ability, or maybe your upbringing. Well-placed triggers that will activate upon entrance to your place of freedom. Now you may interject and think that this is unfair and honestly, I'm not in position to debate fair versus unfair. All I do know is that God himself thought it was necessary. Necessary for a people to endure conflict for the sake of their development. Necessary to experience a place in their life where they'd have to confront the things that could cause them detriment at their next level.

What I drew from the text was that the children of Israel had the desire to be free, and even the boldness to leave but God, in his infinite wisdom, kept them out of a place that was prepared for them, and he did this with a wilderness. According to the text, Israel was not prepared for war, so he sent them into a wilderness. One of God's concerns is that in the face of conflict, a whole nation would abandon the campaign for the freedom that they once cried out for because they were unwilling to fight. I mean, let's put this into context. Is it realistic to think that a nation of slaves, programmed through culture and experience, somehow would, overnight, be ready to launch a military campaign to overtake an occupied land?

Heavens no! God's answer to this dilemma is the wilderness. Truth is, when I set out on the journey to full-time entrepreneurship I was filled with enthusiasm and confidence. I was full of conviction. I thought I was ready! That is, until I was faced with war. While everyone's encounter is different, I would venture to say that no matter who you are, there is a sort of refining, which is life's way of purifying your intentions.

In this place, the wilderness, the fortifying of your character takes place. The wilderness is the place where you discover the price of your destiny and whether you are truly willing to pay it. Up until this point in my journey, I had figured that the desire to become an entrepreneur (or whatever you aspire to) was the sole ingredient in the recipe for success.

Seasoned with my skill set, sprinkle a little time, and shazam, like magic I would be thrust into my desired future in no time. HA... double HA! If that sounds like your train of thought, then I will take the liberty now of derailing it. I submit to you that if it were that simple, then most of the people you know would likely opt to become entrepreneurs and beyond that, more people would be focused on doing what they have the heart to do as opposed to trading time for money in positions they despise every day.

Sadly, this is not the case. Why? There is a price that most people are not willing to pay. There is a war that they are not willing to fight. I want you to take the moment to review what you wrote in Chapter 1. There you mapped the destination and your goal. Here is where I ask the question that may have never entered your mind to ask. What price are you willing to pay to see what you said? Do notjustoverlook this question and read on, intently ponder this.

What I can tell you lies ahead for you is a war. The battlefield will be tailor fit for you. It may challenge you in the realm of finance, like me, or it may be in the realm of doubt (also like me). This list is not exhaustive, and I bet that when your personal war begins you will easily identify it. For me, there came a time when every stream of income I had developed was attacked in sequence.

On-time payments were eventually stretched into a bevy of default payments and accounts that crippled my above seven hundred credit score. I had officially entered the wilderness. A place where the Lord would work out of me the internal threats to my external success. In the wilderness, I believe that the “ore” of your character is tried and refined aside from the pure, untapped potential you possess.

I found that in order to separate the two, that is, the “ore” of my character and the pure potential with which the integrity of my character is fortified, a process is required. Like the refining of pure gold. I think of the wilderness as a place of refining. If you possess the right perspective, you will see it as such as well. I am reminded of a gold-refining process called cupellation, you may not be familiar with the concept, so here is a quick Google definition of one of the methods of gold refinement that I find relevant to our conversation.

Cupellation: A process that has been around since at least the Early Bronze Age, cupellation involves treating ores under high temperatures to separate noble metals, such as gold and silver, from base metals. Base metals, such as copper, zinc, and lead, will oxidize whereas noble metals do not. Cupellation involves melting ore at temperatures over 960 degrees Celsius. At this temperature the base metals oxidize while silver and gold remain on top of the mixture. Most of us, when we think of gold and jewelry, only experience the finished product.

Rarely do we consider the process that it took to make it. Gold in its purest form comes out of the Earth but in order to make it into a product that is shiny and most valuable, built for longevity, the impurities must be taken out. As written above, during cupellation an extreme amount of heat is applied to the raw material. The only thing able to survive depending on the karat is the absolute pure product of gold. The ore or the impurities are not able to stay connected to the pure substance that is intended to be sold and then cherished by the buyer.

The determining factor on how pure your gold is, is dependent on how much heat it withstood in the process. Like gold, those of us in pursuit of our freedom papers are in pursuit of our purest and most valuable form and must also undergo heat and pressure. It is in this place that you can expect challenges to your decision, challenges to your identity, and challenges to your resolve. Without language for what is happening, you will lose sight of the fact that what you are going through is intended to make you the best suited for the market.

The pressure can be so demanding that you would want to forfeit in the place of preparation. It is my earnest hope that after reading this, you will understand that where you are, what you may soon experience, or what you have experienced was not intended to break you.

It was intended to make you into the purest and most valuable version of yourself. I affectionately call this time frame the wilderness because during my wilderness I was encouraged by the children of Israel's journey from slavery to freedom. My wilderness began unknowingly and unexpectedly. It was disrespectful and it did notannounce itself.

It gives you no time to prepare and you typically wander into it. One day you are resolute in your decision, excited about the future, and then the world around you will begin to shake. It may look like a missed check, a missed meal, a meeting that was canceled, or a small, still voice that challenges you on whether you are doing the right thing. Whatever it is, it is just the beginning of a series of events, that though they seem to be fashioned to kill you, have actually been sent to verify the authenticity of your willingness to attain the future you envisioned. The wilderness works the ore out of you.

I thought my wilderness was a satanic attack; I thought every demon in hell had been sent on assignment to touch my finances. I built a system that was meant to feed each other without fail. Each stream was sent to feed the other in a consistent cycle of income. It was the consistency in this system that gave me the assurance to smile when I was laid off. I had long declared independence from the bondage of corporate security, or at least I did so part-time.

But then the wilderness...

When I looked up, I was left with a lot of stress, anxiety, and defeated thinking to go along with my shiny new 425 credit score. To the naked eye, this looks like an attack on finances, it also could be perceived as mismanagement or just a string of nightmarish luck. That could not be further from the truth. This was an exercise, heat, and pressure applied to the area of my trust in God and in what He said.

The fire and the pressure within the form of self-doubting questions, i.e., Are you sure you should be out here? Or bold statements such as just go back to work. This time of unexpected events caused me to reach a mental and emotional threshold, it exposed faulty thinking and faulty beliefs that I had—one of the beliefs being that I trusted God. I had experience with this type of hardship in the past and made the mistake of trying to gauge this new experience based on the last one. The truth is, this situation would cause me to trust Him on a whole new level.

The combination of the shaking and those nagging little voices and ill-timed calls from family members who piled their doubts on top of mine created a mental atmosphere that manifested physically stressful conditions. Soon what showed up was more doubt, heaviness, aggravation, and questioning of the journey.

The pressure exposed these things that were intertwined with the pure purpose of God's will for me. Not only did pressure expose the ore but it started its separation from the purity of what God was trying to do. If you are like me, this time in the wilderness will wear and weigh you down to the point where you will beg to go back to the place where you were.

You will say, "Hey, I got it wrong, no harm, no foul," or "This is for the birds, this just is not it for me." Even more likely is that you will somehow shiftthe blame to God, convincing yourself that he somehow failed you by subjecting you to what you deem as overwhelming pressure. The truth is that God prunes those that bear fruit. Pruning is not a pretty process nor is it painless, but that is not its purpose. I believe some of us have issues making the distinction between the two.

We falsely believe that just because something is purposed, that it should be painless, and nothing could be further from the truth. Consider, if you will, childbirth. There is no more fitting example to my point. To give birth is to submit to the process, all of its discomfort, all of its pains, all of its pressures, and all of the possibilities of complication. I have watched this process a few times and I have come to know that it is highly likely that the only thing keeping that woman from giving up and going home is that she knows that the pain is a part of the process, she knows what giving up will cost and that quitting will not make her any less pregnant.

The only way to get what is inside of her out and birthed into existence is through the painful process of childbirth. By this time, I hope the revelation of the above is hitting you in your chest. You are carrying something that is heaven's idea, and your assignment is to birth it into the earth. The fact that you do not agree with the pain of the wilderness will not make you any less pregnant.

Submitting to the pain and discomfort of the process is the only way to bring forth what God has placed in your heart. The only other option is to knowingly abort, kill, and terminate what you have been g ven to birth. I am not sure about you, but in the days ahead, if God so spares my life, when I am old and gray I do not want to reflect with regret of what I aborted, I want to marvel at what God built. It is here and now that I want you to make the decision that the only thing you will willingly abort is the dea that you will not make it out of the wilderness.

You will fix your eyes on the future and fight for it. There comes a time when you must narrow down your core belief, whether you are spiritual or not. The truth of your life should be rooted in a peace that proves to be a solid foundation no matter what life throws at you. My truth became extremely apparent in the last season in the wilderness. That truth was that God's word was true and that the promise He gave me was indeed for me. Being rooted in that truth meant that no matter what I saw happening around me, no matter what I heard, and no matter what type of external factors came to shake me from my position, that truth remained what it was, the truth.

You must identify the redeeming consistent and foundational truths that you choose to live your life rooted in. Once you have identified those truths you must resolve them in your mind not to be shaken from them. Simply because if what you believe is true then that makes the c rcumstances that seek to negate those things automatically false. Be careful to not root yourself in flimsy truths. My advice is to choose the truth that has yet to fail you. A truth that has stood the testof time, a truth that has withstood persecution, open challenges, and time itself. I will give you one of my truths. I do have a destiny, that destiny is for me, that destiny was spoken from eternity into the present, and that destiny will not die until it is achieved. What is your truth?

Once you have identified your truth you must develop the resolveto rest in it. This is no easy task, there will be constant tests dispatched to purposely undermine where you found your rest. I honestly can say that the only thing that will move you out of your rest is your personal decision to grab hold of what is presented to you and to let go of what you were rooted and rested in.

You must recognize that your truth is your safe place. Once you value your truth as your safe place then you will find yourself clinging to it. Even in times of uncertainty, in times of storm, even in times of turmoil, your truth will cover you. The truth will keep you rooted. The truth will develop in you an endurance that you did not have before. Find your truth.

Throughout the process the Lord would show up with acts of kindness with checks and surprises. It would encourage me and bring something out of me to reignite hope. There was always a provision and a crumb or a little tap or whisper that reminded me he was still there. Something would always come to let me know that even though I was in a difficult spot, I was always in the right spot.

Circumstances can move you into position, and you may not agree with it, but I would have to say that God did not forsake me. Sometimes we do not like the packaging of the promise, but we have to respect it. Much of our anxiety comes from resistance. You have to resolve though, that either he has the next thing planned or my journey ends HERE!

I am telling you that you will have to war for your destiny, your desire, your future, both internally and externally. Understand that the wilderness isn't punishment... it's preparation.

In the space provided, answer these questions: What price are you willing to pay to see what you said you wanted in Chapter 4? What are the truths that you are relying on to keep you rooted in the wilderness?

# TAKE TIME TO REFLECT

# TAKE TIME TO REFLECT

CHAPTER SEVEN

# My Mind Is Made Up

THE SENTIMENTS OF THE LAST chapter are indeed noble and noteworthy, motivational, and may have even revived and rejuvenated your fight. I am grateful for the season and the grace of those words, but something is missing. That something is some practical information that will help you to endure and overcome. I am sure with great effort I could conjure up a few steps with catchy names, but I would be making them up for the sake of filling these lines. Instead, I offer you the one paramount perspective shift that settled me into a resolve that would make the wilderness a little more bearable.

Ok, are you ready? Sit up and pay close attention.

The principle and the most paramount thing that I realized and applied hourly to endure my wilderness was this.

There is only ONE truth. John 16:13 (ESV) When the Spirit of truth comes, he will guide you into all the truth, for he will not speak on his own authority, but whatever he hears he will speak, and he will declare to you the things that are to come. I am going to repeat this to drive home its validity and importance. THERE IS ONLY ONE TRUTH!!!!

Let's dive into this. As a believer, I ascribe to the belief that God is not a man that should lie nor the son of man that He should repent. Whatever the divine speaks, its a sure bet. There is no opportunity for His word to return to him void. In the above scripture reference, the lineage of the spirit of truth originates in the divine, the almighty, the source of all truth.

The function and purpose of the spirit of truth are to echo what has already been stated by the divine. Thus, once I am clear on the instruction and the direction of the divine, then unless there has been a break in the integrity of the information, or a perversion of the source, then what has been spoken is what will occur.

What made this truth so pivotal in surviving the wilderness is that grasping it in context, it meant that everything I encountered while in the wilderness either was sent to assist the word of the Lord in being birthed or it was sent to oppose the word that was spoken by God to shift my focus from what has been deemed infinitely true, to embrace a lie. At the risk of losing you in this train of thought, I offer an illustration.

Peter, who is a popular apostle in scripture, was instructed by Jesus to get out of a boat to perform against all odds an impossible act; he was instructed to walk on water. Peter, like you and me, hears the instruction of the Lord, begins strong, and walks boldly and assuredly. Like us, again, he encounters an external factor that is not in line with his expectation for the journey.

Wind. The scripture declares that when Peter saw the wind, he became afraid, and he sank. What happened to Peter? To the untrained eye, life just happened to Peter, he stepped into a situation and the wind knocked him over. While one might accept that as a logical conclusion having not read the text, I submit to you that, that explanation would not withstand the scrutiny of critical thinking and analysis. Let me try to quickly drive these points and button this up with three small elements that factor into the overall concept that I am attempting to convey.

Matthew 14:22-24; 29 & 30 (NIV): 22 Immediately Jesus made the disciples get into the boat and go on ahead of him to the other side, while he dismissed the crowd. 23 After he had dismissed them, he went up on a mountainside by himself to pray. Later that night, he was there alone, 24 and the boat was already a considerable distance from land, buffeted by the waves because the wind was against it. 29 “Come,” he said. Then Peter got down out of the boat, walked on the water and came toward Jesus. 30 But when he saw the wind, he was afraid and, beginning to sink, cried out, “Lord, save me!”

Beloved friend, the wind was there when Peter decided to step out of the boat. In verse 24, the text clearly states that a considerable amount of wind, tumult, and agitation was present before Peter was even given instruction, before he even received the inspiration to move on the word of God, the wind was present.

This lets us know that 1) God knew what you were up against before He called you to do what He instructed. 2) He had already made calculations for every eternal factor and in the midst of them, His plan still called for your success. You see, before Peter took his very first step out of the boat, he did it with total disregard for the climate he was stepping into. I submit to you that it did not matter because at the start of the journey, Peter’s focus was firmly fixed on the truth, the instruction he had received from God.

The wind was strong when he stepped out, but what kept him was his attachment to the truth. As a matter of fact, it was not until Peter had been getting closer to the goal that he became distracted, which leads me into element number two. In verse 30, Peter takes notice of the wind. An external factor that was present when he started.

It could not sink him or knock him off course as long as he focused on the instruction, but once Peter fixed his attention, his eyes, onto the wind, an external factor, he began to sink. What happened? Peter exchanged the safety and surety of the divinely instructed truth for the raging fallacies of an impotent wind. HE WAS ALREADY THRIVING IN THE MIDST OF THE WIND; IT WAS NOT A THREAT. I will stop here to outline the point of this second element if you are somehow missing it. Count everything that does not serve the future that God showed you as a distraction.

Fixing your focus on these things, whether it be a ding in a credit score, or any other perceived loss, is an agent sent to rob you of progress. It is an empty threat, a fair opportunity cost when considering what you stand to gain. The biggest threat to you not finishing is having a divided mind about whether or not you will. Peter made the mistake of believing that the wind would overpower the word; it never did, it just served to rob him of his focus.

Peter affixed his hope, his belief, and his focus to a powerless possibility and if we are not careful, we will do the same. I noticed that the scripture said that Peter saw the wind. It occurs to me that wind is invisible. What is likely is that Peter saw an invisible wind impacting something else, felt the wind himself, and then panicked. This third element is short and sweet. What I believe triggers Peter is how he felt walking on water with a strong wind blowing against his dry clothes.

I can only imagine the rush of anxiety and fear that overtook him the moment he came to his senses and realized that he had been achieving the impossible. Feelings are nothing more than feelings, feelings are not always accurate measures of the circumstance that you are in. Just because you feel does not mean it is the truth.

You must come to a place where you can discern between your natural emotional response to external stimuli and the truth about how a circumstance affects you. These elements are measures that will help you hold firm to the truth of what was spoken to you when you first stepped out of the boat before you ever encountered a wilderness.

That truth will be tested, and I implore you to use the above elements to test, measure, and validate the thoughts, circumstances, and encounters that will meet you in the wilderness. To close this out, I will give you how I envision this concept. I imagine the truth as a tree that I am affixed to, arms firmly gripping the trunk of that tree with fingers interlocked. Winds blow, and they can be hurricane-force winds that have come to force me to loosen my grip, shift my focus, and rob me of the security of a deeply rooted tree.

I envision myself holding on for dear life to that tree, that truth, knowing full well that if I give in to the raging torrent of the wind I would be utterly lost, confused, and displaced. Stay affixed to the way, affixed to the truth of God's word my friend, and you will make it through any storm.

# TAKE TIME TO REFLECT

# TAKE TIME TO REFLECT

# TAKE TIME TO REFLECT

CHAPTER EIGHT

# Choosing the Right People

AS I CLOSE, I'll leave you with some wisdom on choosing the people that you will allow to help you get to freedom and to eventually free others.

Imagine yourself to be a general contractor. You know there is an order in how you build; no one starts with the roof first, they start at the foundation. And in working in the foundation, you bring in foundation workers, not roof workers. The same could be said for those looking to embark on a new career or new venture or even a new path in life. The people you allow in at the phases of your process and your progress should be appropriate for the level at which you are at. My personal view on this is that you have three groups of people.

The first would be foundation-level people, the second, framing, the third is cosmetics. Foundation-level workers are there to dig in the soil to get in the very raw details of the beginning process. Most people do not know that if you build a house with an unsteady foundation then you will have a nice looking house that won't have any longevity. With that in mind, you want to bring in people that have experience with building firm foundations, ones who have proven themselves to be effective in this area. For you, this looks like mentors and reference points in the forms of people who have been where you want to go or who have wholeheartedly grasped where you are trying to go and are willing to assist.

I would not want apprentice-level foundation builders in charge of advising me on what is best for the house my family or even my tenants would stay in. I would not trust that his or her experience would be abundant enough to accurately avoid potential pitfalls and adequately solve problems that possibly would arrive in the process. An apprentice-level worker may have a base-level knowledge, but odds are they have not built something themselves; they still need the tutelage of an experienced vessel.

At the risk of my point being lost in translation, I will make it plain. When building for your future do not entrust advisement or counsel to those who DO NOT have experience in the specific area, period. Truth be told, sometimes we ask people who have apprentice-level experience about building the next phase of our life.

In my humble opinion, that would be a mistake. Typically, their input and perspective is surface level. Be careful not to let people with surface-level knowledge of the lane that you're trying to enter be on your advisory board. Then you will be at the mercy of their opinions and not cultivated beyond their experience.

There is a difference. This principle in my opinion could be no more vital to invoke than at the foundation level or the genesis of whatever you are trying to start. Choose your foundation workers wisely and surround yourself with a wise and experienced council who are invested in seeing you win, not those who have little more than their opinion to offer. The next level for me will be the framing of your future just like the framing of a house.

This is what sits on top of your foundation, and it will hold the weight of your walls and systems and collaboration with the foundation. At this level in the process, you can be a little less stringent with whom you let in to advise on this level because there is a little more leeway for error, but I'd still use the same blueprint as a rule of thumb.

At this level, I would put up for discussion recommended systems or referrals for companies for you to collaborate with or individuals for you to co-labor with to build or forward your venture.

Lastly, at the cosmetic level, you can be relaxed with these things ,you can change as the seasons go or they remain flexible as times progress. Cosmetic-level input is the perfect place for friends, onlookers. Cosmetics would be paint or the type of vanity you put in a venture. It may be simple input on product choices or leads for a sales call in non-business-related functions. These are things that don't affect the core of what you're trying to do. They can be interchangeable with other substitutions but still work toward your core goal.

Do not bring everyone's opinion into your building. They should know that their opinions are respected but not always necessary. Establish boundaries. The wisdom of who to bring to what level will save you a lot of time, energy, and stress. An equally important thing to know is that consensus is not required for you to move forward. Once you have vision, conviction, and a solid plan, you have the green light to move forward. Do not be a slave to consensus. Understand that not everyone around you sees what you see, shares your outlook, or can execute your vision. To some, what seems impossible is simple to you. If I could sum it up simply, I would say to seek counsel, not approval. People tend to project their fears onto you, so you will need wisdom of who to bring into the mix on what level.

If you are waiting for 100 percent support on your idea, you will never launch because there will always be someone that will find something wrong with what you want to do. Tom may disagree with your product offering, or Sue may not like the color you chose for the logo and letterhead. Randle might despise that you chose to target a specific demographic as opposed to one he suggested. To pursue a life of entrepreneurship, you must be comfortable with being uncomfortable, and with moving forward without the approval of the majority. As a visionary, trust your ability to steward the vision well and to choose people who will do the same.

# TAKE TIME TO REFLECT

# TAKE TIME TO REFLECT

# FINAL THOUGHTS

Here you are, prayerfully equipped with new stamina, new faith, and greater appreciation for the journey, having been given some of the tools for longevity.

At this moment, I can tell you that after the wilderness there is a place of rest. A place I call the buffer. The children of Israel had one, a place where they rested between the wilderness and the promised land. I write you these words from that place in my own life. I know the wilderness is behind me and that what lies ahead is a future that was worth all the headache, stretching, and crushing. It has been my goal with this and the books that will follow to leave behind a blueprint, a map, and a manifesto of my thoughts and experiences as I have ventured to freedom.

I wish I could tell you that what you've read in this book thus far is all you need to see the finish line and to make manifest all that you've set out to do, but I would be misleading you.

These are just some of the keys I can leave behind on the trail as I continue my personal journey. At the time of this writing, understand that this does not contain all the answers, nor will it outline where all the difficulties that you will face are located. You will likely experience the transition from place to place in a multitude of ways and with different challenges, but you will make it if you hold fast to the tools I have given you. So, I leave you with these final words. I am praying for you. My prayer is that you do not faint. That you will not ever believe the lie that God would call you out of a place to abandon you in the middle of it. I pray that you understand the value of the tears that you cried and will cry as you transition.

That you will understand the gravity and the impact that your experience is to have on those who will dare to chase freedom behind you. That the eyes of your understanding will be opened to see that God is not trying to cripple you, He is trying to refine the beauty out of you so that when you emerge from the wilderness—and you will emerge—that you will come forth as pure gold. All this is so, in the name of Jesus (Yeshua). Amen.

As much as it pains me to close, I must leave you for now to tend to the completion of my own journey. I can feel that the completion of these few chapters is symbolic of my own chapter closing on the latest leg of this journey. I sit expectant, grateful, and eager to see what's next so I can tell you all about it.

I want to thank you for allowing me to share my journey.

Until next time. God bless you and keep you. Dre.

# AFTERWORD

My hope and prayer are that what is written here will be beneficial to you both naturally and spiritually. As in a hospital setting, once you are discharged, you receive your paperwork. That processing can be quite daunting because you already have receipts of the news of why you arrived in the first place. So, here the doctor gives you scripts, after care, and maybe a few more pieces of paper before sending you on your way.

I am discharging you, in this moment, with the charge that you will take this manual and change the world. Before you go forth and change the world, I want you to start with yourself. I want you to start internally, mentally, emotionally, and physically. Another type of journey to external freedom is wholeness.

Make sure you are equipped to handle all you believe will take place in your life. It is heavy and weighty, but you will understand the reason of its necessity. What you are building is not just about your now, but about future generations. Even more important are the lessons, the traditions, and the memories that have made up what you call life. Like the discharge paperwork you receive, what you do with what you have received is super important.

Take my story and my journey and utilize every lesson as you navigate your own journey. Although not the same, there are some default situations that will help you. You are free now! Stamped and approved to go forth and become all you were created to be and everything you have ever dreamed you would be. Go!

Made in the USA
Columbia, SC
14 January 2024

30344950R00050